WITHDRAWN

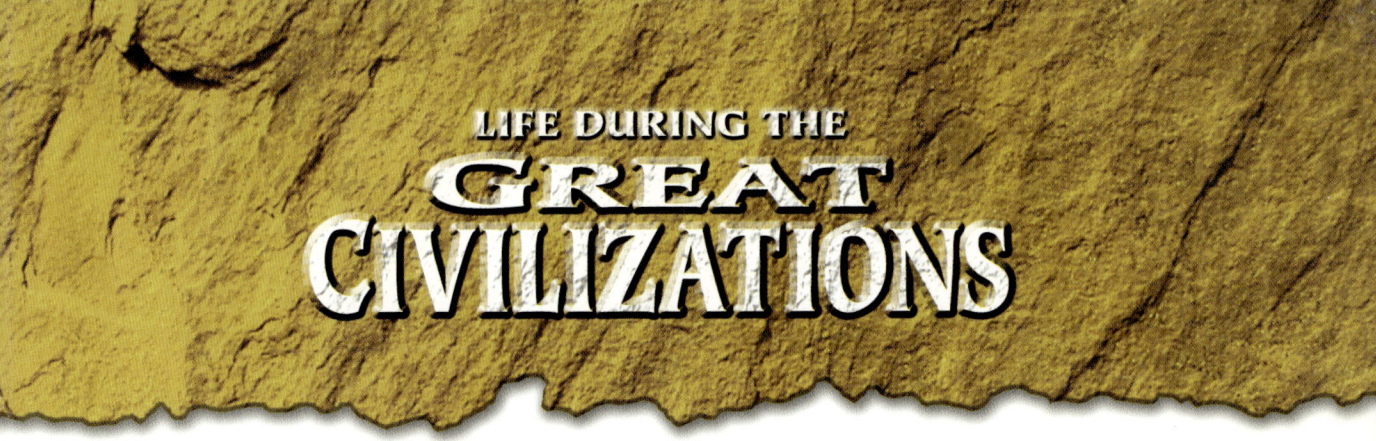

Ancient Rome

Don Nardo

BLACKBIRCH® PRESS

San Diego • Detroit • New York • San Francisco • Cleveland • New Haven, Conn. • Waterville, Maine • London • Munich

© 2003 by Blackbirch Press™. Blackbirch Press™ is an imprint of The Gale Group, Inc., a division of Thomson Learning, Inc.

Blackbirch Press™ and Thomson Learning™ are trademarks used herein under license.

For more information, contact
The Gale Group, Inc.
27500 Drake Rd.
Farmington Hills, MI 48331-3535
Or you can visit our Internet site at http://www.gale.com

ALL RIGHTS RESERVED
No part of this work covered by the copyright hereon may be reproduced or used in any form or by any means—graphic, electronic, or mechanical, including photocopying, recording, taping, Web distribution or information storage retrieval systems—without the written permission of the publisher.

Every effort has been made to trace the owners of copyrighted material.

Photo credits on page 47.

LIBRARY OF CONGRESS CATALOGING-IN-PUBLICATION DATA

Nardo, Don, 1947-
  Ancient Rome / by Don Nardo.
    p. cm. — (Life during the great civilizations)
  Includes bibliographical references and index.
  Contents: The Roman social ladder — Houses and family relationships — Rome's multitude of gods — Roads and aqueducts make life easier.
    ISBN 1-56711-742-2 (hardback : alk. paper)
  1. Rome—Social life and customs—Juvenile literature. [1. Rome—Social life and customs. 2. Rome—Civilization.] I. Title. II. Series.

DG78.N355 2003
937—dc21   2003008271

Printed in United States
10 9 8 7 6 5 4 3 2 1

Contents

INTRODUCTION 5
Many Different Roman Societies

CHAPTER ONE 9
The Roman Social Ladder

CHAPTER TWO 17
Houses and Family Relationships

CHAPTER THREE 25
Rome's Multitude of Gods

CHAPTER FOUR 33
Roads and Aqueducts Make Life Easier

NOTES 40
GLOSSARY 41
FOR MORE INFORMATION 43
INDEX 45
PICTURE CREDITS 47
ABOUT THE AUTHOR 48

INTRODUCTION

Many Different Roman Societies

Ancient Roman society existed for a very long time. According to legend, Rome was founded in 753 B.C., but archaeologists have found evidence that villages existed on some of the city's seven hills as early as 1000 B.C.

At first, kings ruled Rome. Then, in 509 B.C., the leading citizens threw out the kings and established the Roman Republic. It was run by a powerful legislature—the Senate—and officials elected by an assembly made up of citizens. In the centuries that followed, the armies of the republic conquered most of the Mediterranean world. In the first century B.C., however, these armies turned on each other. A series of disastrous civil wars rocked the Roman world, and the republic fell. The final victor of these wars, Augustus, created a new Roman government based on one-man rule—the Roman Empire.

Opposite Page: The ruins of Rome's main Forum, where the city's public buildings stood, survive today.

The Roman realm reached its height of size and splendor during the empire's first two centuries. Then it steadily declined. Ultimately, invasions of tribal peoples from northern Europe overran the empire, and the last Roman emperor was forced to step down from his throne in A.D. 476.

Thus, Roman civilization existed for nearly fifteen hundred years. During these centuries, it underwent enormous changes. Rome went from a small, crude town with wooden shacks and muddy streets to a huge city with paved streets and magnificent stone buildings. The people, as well as the way they lived, changed, too. At first, they were culturally backward farmers who could not read and disdained most forms of luxury. Over time, however, many Romans became literate, worldly, and fond of creature comforts. Social customs also changed dramatically. For example, women started out with few civil rights, but

This reconstruction shows what the northern part of the Forum looked like during the Empire.

This nineteenth-century drawing shows some typical ancient Roman clothing styles.

eventually they gained many rights and a stronger voice in society. Also, Rome imported new gods from many lands, which greatly expanded religious diversity.

Over the centuries, therefore, many different Roman societies existed, each with its own political, economic, and social realities. Everyday life was considerably different in each of these societies. This book captures a brief snapshot of the way people lived during the early years of the empire, when Rome was strong, secure, and vibrant. It is a picture of a proud, industrious, religiously devout people who truly believed it was their destiny to rule the world forever.

CHAPTER ONE

The Roman Social Ladder

Augustus, the first ruler of the Roman Empire, was widely respected and loved by his subjects. When he died in A.D. 14, more than a hundred thousand people attended his funeral. They marched through the city's streets in a solemn parade that stretched for miles.

Those in the ranks of this great crowd came from all walks of life and presented a cross section of Roman society—rich and poor, male and female, and free and slave. A person's position in the parade reflected his or her social standing. The people who enjoyed the highest social status and authority marched in the front ranks and carried the emperor's coffin. Slaves marched in the rear.

Strict distinctions among social classes at such formal events was no accident. Roman society was deeply concerned with social status and rankings. In a way, it resembled a tall ladder, with the wealthiest, most powerful people on the highest rungs and the poorest, least powerful people on the lowest ones. Naturally, people on the lower rungs wanted to move higher up the ladder. This was difficult, however. Those who tried to raise their status found many obstacles in their path. For this reason, only a small minority of lower-class Romans ever managed to become members of the privileged classes. In general, most people simply accepted Rome's rigid class structure and its inequalities as inevitable.

Opposite Page: This large statue is of Augustus, founder and first ruler of the Roman Empire.

People of all walks of life milled about Rome's hub, the main Forum.

The Upper Classes

On the top rung of the social ladder were the patricians. They were a small group of very rich men (and their wives and children) whose wealth came from large farming estates. They did not work on their farms, however, as poor Roman farmers did. By the early empire, most patricians lived primarily in elegant townhouses in Rome or in other cities. They hired caretakers to manage their country estates, and they collected the profits these farms produced.

Wealth and freedom from menial work were not the only privileges the patricians enjoyed. They held great prestige and influence in society. It was widely accepted that they possessed an inborn moral authority, called *auctoritas* in Latin, the language the Romans spoke. This authority entitled them to rule or judge the members of the lower classes. Most senators were patricians, for example, and the first five emperors came from patrician families. The first-century B.C. senator and orator Cicero explained why it was both natural and good for men like himself to rule:

> What situation can be more splendid than the government [in the hands of men of] excellence and virtue? ... The ignorance and rashness of the masses have caused [power to be transferred] from the many to the few. ... When such men [as the patricians] watch over the state, the citizens must necessarily be very happy and blessed.[1]

Not far beneath the patricians on the social ladder were the equestrians, or knights. These were well-to-do persons whose money came from business, trade, and other financial dealings rather than from land. Most equestrian men engaged in professions such as banking, money lending, tax collecting, and importing and exporting various goods. It was very difficult for a lower-class person to enter the equestrian order. One had to demonstrate a net worth of at least four hundred thousand sesterces, about four hundred times the annual salary of a Roman soldier.

Slaves carried wealthy Romans in litters, one of the luxuries of the upper classes.

The Senate was the republic's leading governmental branch.

The Lower Classes

Well below the patricians and equestrians were the members of the lower classes, who made up the vast majority of the population. They were divided into three broad groups. The first consisted of freeborn Romans, or freemen. They were citizens, so they possessed basic civil rights, including the right to plead a case in court. They held a wide variety of jobs, but most were farmers, soldiers, shopkeepers, or ordinary laborers.

The other two groups that made up the lower classes were slaves and freedmen (former slaves). In earlier centuries, most slaves were non-Italian people captured during wars. By the early empire, however, a majority were born of slave parents in slave-owning homes or were purchased from slave traders. Slaves did almost all of the menial and dirty jobs in Roman society. They worked in mines and fields, cooked, washed clothes, and cleaned houses, streets, and toilets. On the other hand, some slaves, especially Greeks, were educated. They sometimes worked as financial managers, shop clerks, tailors, bakers, and innkeepers.

One of the most common and respected professions in Rome was soldiering.

Some slaves earned their freedom. On occasion, a kind master freed a slave as a reward for long years of faithful service. Other slaves bought their freedom with money saved up from the small allowance that many masters granted their slaves. Either way, freedmen played vital roles in society. Some worked as artisans, shopkeepers, and farm managers. Others were teachers, secretaries, traders, and musicians and other entertainers. Their social status remained little better than that of slaves, however. Most freeborn Romans simply refused to accept former slaves as equals, no matter how talented, hardworking, and honest they might be.

Patrons and Clients

Thus, vast differences in wealth, status, and influence divided the Roman classes. Yet all of these groups were tightly connected by one of society's most important institutions—the patronage system. It was based on an exchange of services between two parties. The first, called the client, was someone in need. He or she depended in one way or another on a person who was more influential or powerful, called the patron. Usually, the client did various favors for the patron. Among others, these included running errands or showing up at court to support a patron's legal case. As a reward, the client received legal or financial protection or invitations to banquets at the patron's home.

Some patrons took advantage of the situation. They demanded weekly and even daily favors of their clients and

Most of the actors who performed in Roman theaters were freedmen.

offered only an occasional free meal to repay the debt. The first-century A.D. humorist Juvenal, a man of modest means, bitterly joked,

> Get one thing clear from the start. A dinner invitation settles the score in full for all your earlier services.... Each meal, however, infrequent, your patron reckons against you to square his accounts. So if, after two months' neglect... he says 'Be my guest'... you're beside yourself with joy.[2]

Not all clients were from the lower classes. The patronage system existed at all levels of Roman society. Although a wealthy person had many clients, he or she was often a client of an even richer and more powerful individual. All through the empire, for example, wealthy people sought and sometimes obtained the emperor's patronage. Patronage, therefore, was a sort of social glue that forced the various classes to interact and stay on reasonably good terms.

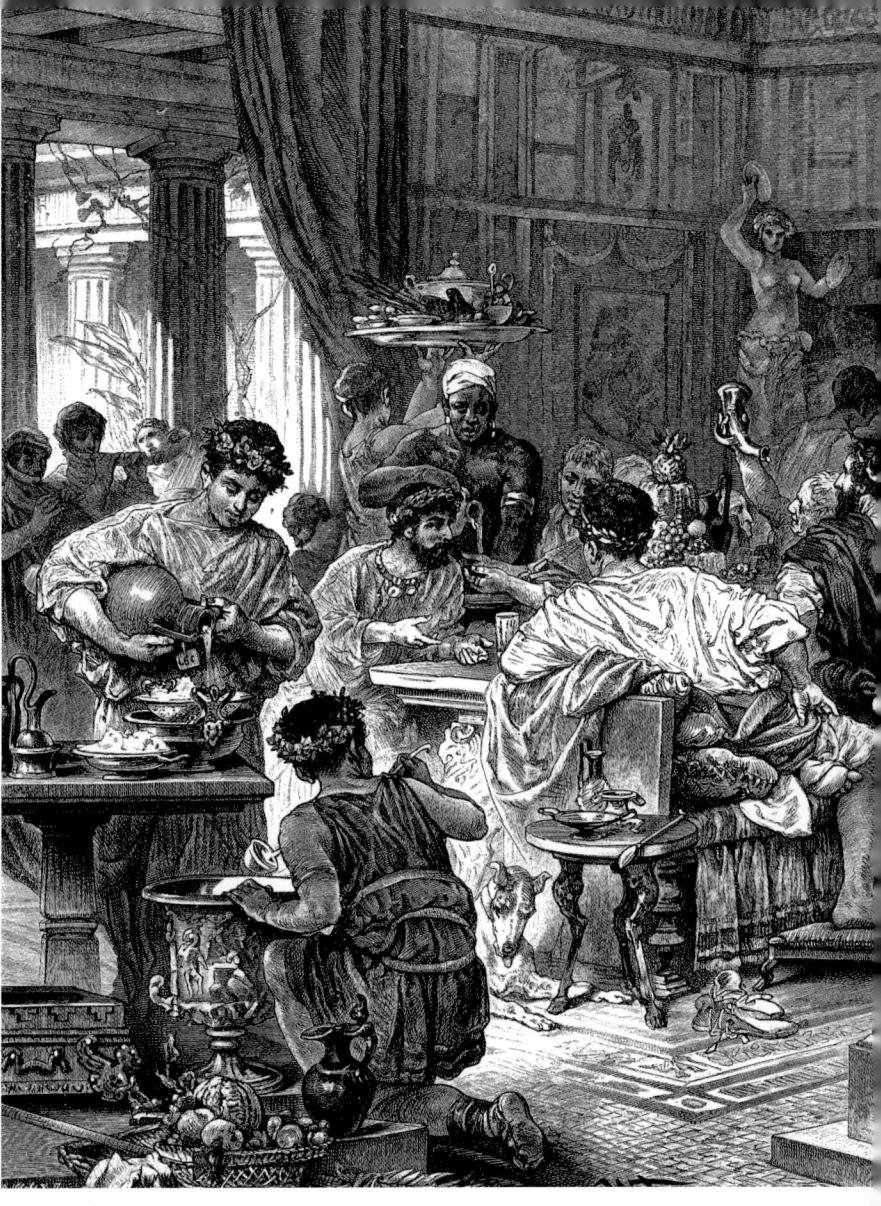

In this illustration, slaves serve the guests at a lavish dinner in a private Roman home.

CHAPTER TWO

Houses and Family Relationships

The Roman home and family were closely connected. In fact, the Latin word for family, *familia*, translates literally as "household." To the Romans, the family was not just the group of people who lived in a home. The term usually had a much broader meaning. In addition to parents, children, and other relatives, the family included the house itself and all the furnishings and other property inside. The household slaves were also part of the family. So was the father's and mother's heritage, which included the tombs of deceased relatives and busts and other images of them.

The household was also a sacred place because it was thought to contain a number of invisible spirits that guarded the family, its hearth, and its food supplies. Each home had a private altar as well, at which the family members prayed to the gods. "Here are [a Roman's] altars," Cicero wrote about the household. "Here are his hearths, here are his household gods. Here, all his sacred rites, all of his religious ceremonies are preserved."[3] This means that a Roman house was more than a mere place to live. It was also a holy spot.

Country Homes

The size and layout of such houses in the early empire varied, depending on various factors. In the countryside, farming families of average or less than average means dwelled

Opposite Page: Roman families included not only the living members but also the deceased, who were memorialized by their tombs and by images of them.

in small cottages or huts. Some of these stood by themselves on a patch of farmland. Others clustered together in small villages. The poorer huts were made of wood, although many were constructed of fieldstones. Most had from one to three small rooms and were sparsely furnished. The floors consisted of beaten dirt, sometimes covered by straw mats, wooden planks, or small stone blocks. A raised hearth in the middle of the main room provided warmth and a place to cook.

The country houses of the well-to-do were called villas. These were much larger than ordinary farmers' huts and usually rested at the centers of large estates. Such residences were elegantly furnished and featured fountains, statues, and well-tended gardens. Even a small villa had six to ten rooms. Most often they were grouped around a rectangular inner courtyard that was open to the weather. Some villas were true mansions. In a letter, the wealthy first-century A.D. diplomat Pliny

A Roman wall painting depicts a large villa in the countryside.

The atrium of a wealthy Roman's townhouse might be decorated with columns and paintings.

the Younger described one of his villas. It had an entrance hall, kitchen, and four dining rooms, he said. There were also several meeting rooms, five bedrooms, a library, four bathing rooms, a handball court, swimming pool, and ample servants' quarters.

City Residences

Like its country counterpart, a well-to-do city family also lived in a luxurious home, called a *domus*, or townhouse.

Through the front door, a person entered a front hall, called the atrium, which was decorated with columns, statues, and wall paintings. It was here that the owner received his clients, who arrived each morning to see what errands he needed them to run. From the atrium, corridors led away to other rooms. These included the kitchen, master's study, one or more dining rooms, bedrooms, and servants' chambers.

There was also a bathroom. It featured a toilet with pipes (made of ceramics, lead, or bronze) that carried wastes away to the city sewer. Some of these bathrooms also had tubs. The water came from faucets

Pliny Describes His Villa

The first-century A.D. diplomat and letter writer Pliny the Younger left behind a lengthy description of his villa near Ostia (Rome's port city). It reads in part,

> The house … opens into a hall … and then there are two colonnades [rows of columns] … which enclose a small but pleasant courtyard. This makes a splendid retreat in bad weather, being protected by windows and still more by the overhanging roof. Opposite the middle of it is a cheerful inner hall, and then a dining room.… To the left of this… is a large bedroom and then another smaller one which lets in the morning sunshine.… Round the corner is a room … with one wall fitted with shelves like a library to hold the books which I read and read again.

and pipes that tapped into nearby aqueducts, large artificial channels that carried water from the countryside into the city.

The vast majority of city dwellers could not afford such luxuries. They lived mostly in large apartment blocks called *insulae*. The average *insula* was three to five stories tall and had rows of shops, taverns, and snack bars on the ground floor. The other floors were filled with apartments. A few, usually on the second story, were large and catered to the well-to-do. A surviving rental ad reads, "The Arrius Pollio Apartment Complex. ... FOR RENT from July 1, streetfront shops with counter space, luxurious second-story apartments. Prospective renters, please make arrangements with Primus, slave of [the owner]."[4]

Most of the apartments in an *insula* were tiny and had few conveniences. For example, there were no pipes to bring in water or carry away wastes. That meant that the occupants had to carry their water in buckets up two, three, or more flights of stairs. (The water came

Most city dwellers lived in insulae, *multistory apartment buildings designed much like the model pictured, with shops and taverns on the ground floor.*

from public fountains that connected with the aqueducts.) They also had to carry their wastes out in buckets and dump them into the sewers. Another problem was that such buildings were often badly constructed. Fires were common, and from time to time, part or all of an apartment block collapsed, causing death and injury.

Fathers, Mothers, and Slaves

Whatever kind of house and luxuries a family could afford, basic relationships between family members were the same everywhere. The head of the household was the paterfamilias. His word was final on all matters dealing with the *familia*. A few fathers were overly strict or even abusive in dealing with family members. On the other hand, many were even tempered and kind and earned great respect. The Roman poet Horace penned this tribute to own father:

This Roman man and his wife are depicted in a wall painting in their home.

[If] all my life was pure and innocent … my father was the reason. So he reared me. Poor he was…. Yet he [made sure that I received a good education].... For all this now, what praise can I bestow on him, much greater than the thanks I owe?[5]

The lady of the house, the materfamilias, was either the paterfamilias's wife or, if he was not married, his mother. The duties she and her daughters performed varied according to the family's wealth. Poor women not only cooked, made clothes, and did most of the chores, but they also worked outside the home. (Some

Masters and slaves traded places during the Saturnalia in December.

toiled in the fields. Others were barmaids, clothes makers, or laundresses.) In wealthier homes, women sometimes made clothes, but they spent much of their time supervising the household finances and slaves.

The slaves did most of the actual labor, which included cleaning, cooking and serving meals, tending the hearths, sewing, and making repairs. Some household slaves suffered harsh discipline, beatings, or even sexual abuse. Most received humane treatment, however. In particular, slaves born in the home, known as *vernae*, sometimes enjoyed care and affection similar to that of the master's own children.

Household slaves also looked forward to holidays, when the master was apt to be in a good mood and give them extra privileges. Best of all was the Saturnalia, a festival celebrated in December. Following custom, masters and slaves switched places for a day. The master cooked and waited on the slaves hand and foot while the slaves sat back and barked orders. Ironically, a slave in an upper-class Roman household often had a more comfortable, secure life than a poor free person.

CHAPTER THREE

Rome's Multitude of Gods

Religion was one of the cornerstones of ancient Roman society. Most Romans devoutly believed in a multitude of divine spirits and gods (although a few doubted the existence of these beings). The Romans were also unusually tolerant of new gods and religious ideas. It was customary, for example, to adopt the gods and worship of the peoples whom Rome conquered. There was even a formula the commanding general recited to welcome such a god. "To you I pray," he chanted. "I respectfully ask [you] to abandon [this] people and city … and to come to me and my people.… I ask that … you may take under your protection me and the people of Rome."[6]

This spirit of acceptance displayed by the Romans in religious matters was based on a simple idea—all faiths were equal paths leading to the same place. The concept was best expressed by a Roman nobleman named Symmachus:

> The divine Mind has distributed different guardians … to different cities.… All worship should be considered as one. We look on the same stars … [and] the same world surrounds us. What difference does it make by what pains each seeks the truth?[7]

Rome's Sacred Pantheon Grows

When it came to accepting foreign gods, the Romans were particularly impressed with those of the Greeks. Over time, Rome borrowed some gods directly from the Greeks. The

Opposite Page: The Pantheon building (interior pictured) housed images of the many gods that made up the Roman pantheon.

A wall painting shows the love goddess Venus with her son, Eros.

first of these was Asclepius, the Greek god of medicine and healing. A party of Romans traveled to Greece, found a famous, sacred statue of the god, and carefully transported it back to Rome. There, it was widely worshiped under its slightly changed Latin name—Aesculapius.

In many other cases, a Greek god reminded the Romans of one of their own local Italian deities. The Romans assumed, therefore, that the two gods were one and the same. In this way, they came to identify their ancient sky god, Jupiter, with the leader of the Greek gods, Zeus. The old Roman agricultural god, Mars, took on the attributes of the Greek Ares, god of war, and so forth.

In their Greco-Roman form, Jupiter and Mars became part of Rome's official state religion. Another member of this pantheon, or group of gods, was Juno, Jupiter's wife and the protector of women and childbirth. Some others included Neptune, ruler of the seas; Minerva, goddess of war and the protector of craftsmen; and Venus, goddess of love. The government wanted to make sure that these deities continued to show favor to Rome. For that reason, it erected temples for them and honored them in public rituals conducted during yearly religious festivals.

The Rituals of Worship

Although most Romans accepted the existence of these gods, the average person did not actively worship all of them. Instead, various individuals and groups chose to worship one or a select few on a regular basis. Whichever god or gods one favored, the rituals of worship were basically the same. In performing them, the worshiper entered into a kind of contract, with the deity. This deal was called *do ut des*, which meant, "I, the mortal, give to you, the god, so that you may give back to me."

The two principal rituals of worship were sacrifice and prayer. In sacrifice, the worshiper offered a gift to a god, usually something that would nourish the deity. Often it was an animal, such as a cow, sheep, goat, or pig. By tradition, male deities received offerings of male animals and female deities received offerings of female animals. The worshipers led the animal, called the victim, to an altar. The altar was

An early sketch shows Roman women sacrificing spices to a god.

usually located outside on the grounds of a temple. (No sacrifice or other major ceremony took place inside the building so as to respect the god's privacy.)

At the altar, the worshipers sprinkled salt, wine, flour, or a sacred cake over the victim's head. This was to purify the animal, to make it clean and acceptable in the god's eyes. Then a priest cut the victim's throat. The blood drained into a bowl. Next, the priest and his assistants carefully cut up the animal and tossed the bones and fat into a fire burning on the altar. The belief was that the smoke rose up and nourished the god. The meat and organs from the victim were cooked and eaten by the worshipers in a sacred feast that followed the sacrifice. It was crucial to perform all these steps correctly. If a single mistake was made, it was believed that the god would refuse the sacrifice.

The other major ritual, prayer, also followed strict rules. Almost always, a person prayed standing up and spoke to the god aloud. The person first called out the god's name, then listed the deity's powers and known achievements. Finally, the worshiper asked for the god's assistance. As in sacrifice, even a small mistake in the order or wording of these steps required that the worshiper go back to the beginning and repeat them. Juvenal suggested that many people prayed for the wrong things, such as wealth, political power, or military glory. It was better, he said, to pray for "a sound mind in a sound body, courage not to fear death … and above all, virtue."[8]

Early Christian Rituals

Prayer was a central pillar of worship for another of the many faiths that grew in the lands controlled by Rome—Christianity. That faith was just getting started during the early empire. At the time, most Roman Christians kept to themselves and worshiped in secret. The main day of worship was Sunday, but ceremonies occurred on Wednesday and

Foreign Gods Accepted in Rome

Cybele, the "Great Mother" goddess of Asia Minor depicted by this statue, was one of the foreign deities adopted by the Romans.

When other foreign gods later made their way to Rome, they were accepted and respected alongside the state gods. The new arrivals had their own temples and festivals. The Romans welcomed Mithras, an important Persian god, and from Asia Minor (what is now Turkey) came Cybele, the "Great Mother." Syria gave Rome the half-human, half-fish goddess called Atargatis. One of the most popular of all the imported deities was Isis, from Egypt, who brought fertility and purified people's sins. In his novel The Golden Ass, the Roman writer Apuleius describes her popular image:

She had a full head of hair that hung down ... and flowed gently over her divine neck.... [Her] crown was held in place by coils of rearing snakes ... and it was adorned above with waving ears of corn. She wore a multicolored dress woven from fine linen, one part of which shone radiantly white.

Friday as well. On Friday, Christians went without food to observe Jesus Christ's betrayal by Judas and the crucifixion.

Usually, an early Christian Sunday service began with the worshipers praying and singing hymns. Then everyone listened to a long reading from the Scriptures, or Old Testament. Finally came the main part of the service—the ceremony of communion. The worshipers ate bread and drank wine, which stood for Christ's body and blood. In some parts of the empire, communion took place at the tombs of deceased Christians in underground cemeteries. The worshipers believed that this helped to join together the spirits of the living and the dead. Christians around the world still take part in these rituals. This means that a vital aspect of life and worship in the early Roman Empire still thrives.

Early Christians used bread and wine for the communion ceremony.

The Growth and Survival of Christianity

Christianity first took root in the Roman province of Judaea in Palestine. About A.D. 30, a Jewish preacher, Jesus of Nazareth, was executed by

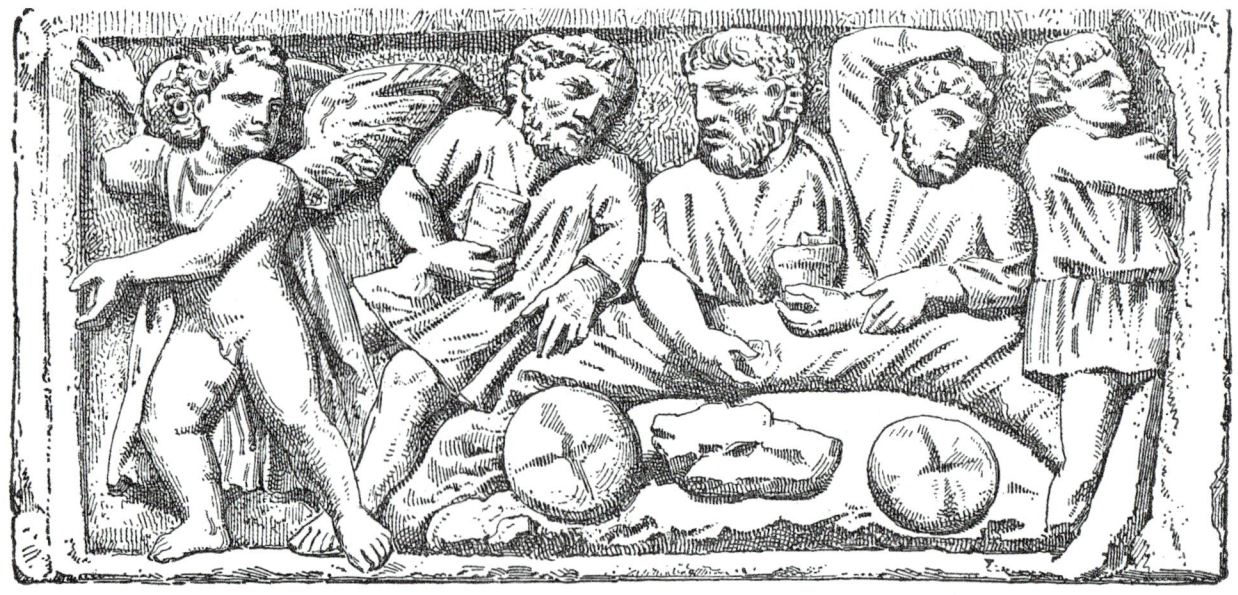

During a persecution, Christians (at right) were tied to stakes and burned.

the Romans. In the belief that he was the son of the god worshiped by the Jews, his followers kept his memory and teachings alive. Later in the same century, the Christians began to gain non-Jewish converts and separated from Judaism (the religion of the Jews). Unlike the adherents of other new faiths, however, the Christians found themselves scorned rather than accepted by most Romans. It was not because the Christians believed in a different god. One problem was that they refused to recognize other people's gods, which the Romans saw as rude and insulting. Also, a rumor spread that the Christians killed babies in their secret rituals. Another rumor said that they hated the human race.

These rumors turned out to be mistaken. At the time, however, most people believed them, so the Roman government began to persecute the Christians. Only much later did the Christians prevail. They managed to survive the persecutions and slowly grew in numbers. In the fourth century, the emperors themselves began to convert, and Christianity became the new state religion. Later, after the fall of Rome, Christianity survived and went on to become one of the world's major faiths.

CHAPTER FOUR

Roads and Aqueducts Make Life Easier

The state of technology in the ancient world, including the Roman Empire, was primitive. There was no electricity, so people used torches and oil-burning lamps to see at night. With no telephones, faxes, or the Internet, the Romans had to communicate through hand-carried messages. They also lacked complex machines. All work had to be done by the muscle power of humans or animals, aided by wheels and some simple pulleys and levers. All travel was by foot, donkey, wagon, or ship, so it took days and sometimes weeks or months to reach distant locations.

To some degree, the Romans made up for these limitations. They did this partly through new and inventive ideas. Mostly, however, they took older, simple ideas and applied them, through hard work and brute force, on a grand scale. They built thousands of miles of paved roads to make travel easier, for example. They also erected dozens of aqueducts to supply millions of people with freshwater.

In fact, the Romans were by far the greatest engineers and builders of the ancient world. Moreover, most of their construction projects had very practical uses. One of Rome's water commissioners in the early empire, Sextus Julius Frontinus, expressed pride in this achievement. Citing the aqueducts, he wrote, "With such an array of indispensable structures carrying so many waters, compare, if you will, the idle [Egyptian] Pyramids or the useless, though famous, works of the Greeks!"[9]

Opposite Page: This ancient Roman road was so well constructed it is still in use.

Water for Drinking, Cooking, and Bathing

Frontinus had good reason to be proud of the aqueducts he managed. In his day, nine of these engineering marvels supplied water to the empire's capital city. Each consisted of a complex series of channels, bridges, tunnels, pools, pipes, fountains, and nozzles. Their combined daily output was about 200 million gallons. That was enough to supply each resident of Rome with two hundred gallons of water a day.

To build an aqueduct was laborious and time consuming. First, surveyors located a water source, such as a spring, in the nearby mountains. Then they marked out the miles-long course for the *specus*, the channel through which the water flowed. Most of this channel lay underground. This required digging many long trenches

This well-preserved arcade for a Roman aqueduct is in Spain.

Sections of lead pipe from one of Rome's many aqueducts survive today.

and tunnels with picks and shovels, work accomplished by large gangs of slaves Where needed, the engineers erected tall stone bridges called arcades to carry the *specus* aboveground. All along the way, the channel had a very slight downward incline. That way, the natural power of gravity caused the water to flow in the desired direction.

At the aqueduct's frontend, where it reached the city, the channel divided and became part of a complicated water distribution system. First, the water was purified by two means. It passed through metal grills, which filtered out large particles. Then the water entered some large tanks, where smaller impurities settled to the bottom.

Next, the clean water entered numerous pipes. Special manuals gave instructions in the proper construction of pipes. The Roman architect Vitruvius, for instance, wrote that ceramic pipes "are to be made not less than two inches thick.... The joints are to be coated with quicklime worked up with oil."[10]

Such pipes carried the water to bathhouses, the wealthier homes, and public fountains. The main function of these fountains was not decorative. Rather, average Romans drew water from them for drinking, cooking, and bathing. In most places in the city, the fountains were installed no more than 260 feet apart to minimize the difficulty of carrying water in buckets for long distances.

Building the Road System

No less impressive than the aqueducts was Rome's vast system of roads. In the early empire, about three hundred paved or partially paved roads crisscrossed the realm. Their total length was almost fifty thousand miles! Meanwhile, thousands of smaller unpaved but well-maintained roads branched out from the main routes. The road system made sending an army to a faraway trouble spot much faster and easier. It also allowed traders, construction crews, diplomats, letter carriers, and ordinary people to travel more quickly and comfortably.

Milestones like this one were erected at intervals along Roman roads.

To construct a large paved road was very expensive and required the services of large numbers of people. First, surveyors marked out the proposed route. Next, crews of slaves cleared the route of rocks, trees, and other obstacles.

Punishment for Vandals and Thieves

The water commissioner Frontinus penned a volume titled The Aqueducts of Rome, which has survived. In it, he cites the legal penalties for tampering with or damaging the aqueducts. This included water thieves, people who diverted water for their private use.

> Whoever [shall] … pierce or break the channels, conduits, arches, pipes, tubes, reservoirs, or basins of the public waters . . . or who shall do damage with intent to prevent water-courses, or any portions of them, from going, falling, flowing, reaching, or being conducted into the city of Rome … shall be condemned to pay a fine of 100,000 sestertii to the Roman people.… Further, whoever is or shall be water commissioner … is authorized to fine, bind over by bail, or restrain the offender.

Engineers then supervised the laying of the roadbed, which had to rest on material firm enough to support heavy traffic over long periods of time. The workers dug a trench, on average three feet deep and twenty-three feet wide. They filled the bottom of the trench with large stones mixed with sand or clay. Over this layer went a second one composed of pebbles and gravel. Finally came the paving stones, cut into rectangular slabs or irregular ones that fit together like the pieces of a jigsaw puzzle.

Such a road had several added features. It was cambered, for example, which meant that it was curved so that its middle was slightly higher than its sides. That way, rainwater flowed off the road and into drainage ditches. Some roads also had artificial ruts carved into them to help guide the wheels of wagons and chariots. In addition, the builders erected milestones at intervals along the roadside. These stone markers bore useful information for travelers, such as the distances between the markers and nearby cities.

Services Along the Roads

The major Roman roads also featured many services for travelers of all kinds. Every seven to twelve miles, mounted letter carriers and traders could find posting stations. These were stables that repaired broken

This Roman street features curbstones and carved tracks for chariot wheels.

The ruins of an arcade from a Roman aqueduct grace the Turkish countryside.

wagons, cared for horses and donkeys, and supplied fresh animals when needed.

There were also inns along the main roads, usually located at intervals of about twenty to thirty miles. These establishments were often named after animals (for example, the Elephant), weapons (the Sword), and gods (the Neptune). Most featured a large kitchen and dining room and a stable as well as rooms to rent.

Some of the busier intersections of the major highways featured more than just inns. Over time, some travelers decided to settle down and built homes, restaurants, markets, bathhouses, and religious shrines at such junctions. These often continued to expand into towns. In this way, the roads helped to spread Roman civilization and its customs and ideals to most regions of the known world. As the great Roman scholar Pliny the Elder put it,

> Now that world-wide communications have been established thanks to the authority of the Roman Empire ... living standards [across the world] have been improved by the interchange of goods and by ... the general availability of things previously [unavailable].[11]

Notes

Chapter 1: The Roman Social Ladder

1. Cicero, "On the Republic," in *As the Romans Did: A Sourcebook in Roman Social History*, ed. Jo Ann Shelton. New York: Oxford University Press, 1988, pp. 10–11.
2. Juvenal, *Satires*. Published as *The Sixteen Satires*, trans. Peter Green. New York: Penguin, 1974, p. 117.

Chapter 2: Houses and Family Relationships

3. Cicero, "On His House," in *The Orations of Marcus Tullius Cicero*, trans. C.D. Yonge. London: George Bell, 1891, p. 182.
4. Quoted in Shelton, *As the Romans Did*, p. 64.
5. Quoted in Francis R.B. Godolphin, ed., *The Latin Poets*. New York: Random House, 1949, pp. 296–97.

Chapter 3: Rome's Multitude of Gods

6. Quoted in Shelton, *As the Romans Did*, pp. 369–70.
7. Quoted in Brian Tierney, ed., *The Middle Ages*, vol. 1, *Sources of Medieval History*. New York: Knopf, 1973, pp. 23–24.
8. Quoted in Meyer Reinhold, *Essentials of Greek and Roman Classics*. Great Neck, NY: Barron's, 1946, pp. 318–19.

Chapter 4: Roads and Aqueducts Make Life Easier

9. Sextus Julius Frontinus, "The Aqueducts of Rome," in *The Stratagems and the Aqueducts of Rome*, trans. C.E. Bennett. Cambridge, MA: Harvard University Press, 1993, pp. 357–59.
10. Vitruvius, *On Architecture*, vol. 2, trans. Frank Granger. Cambridge, MA: Harvard University Press, 1962, pp. 137–41.
11. Pliny the Elder, "Natural History," in *Pliny the Elder: Natural History: A Selection*, trans. John H. Healy. New York: Peguin Books, 1991, p. 182.

Glossary

aqueduct: An artificial channel that carried water from the countryside into a city.

arcade: A bridge supported by a row of arches, usually made of stone. Arcades carried both roads and water channels.

archaeologist: A scholar who digs up and studies the ruins and artifacts of past cultures.

atrium: The front hall or foyer of a Roman house.

auctoritas: Moral authority.

cambered: Slightly curved so that the middle is higher than the sides, as in the case of a paved road.

client: See patronage.

communion: A Christian ceremony in which the worshipers eat bread and drink wine, which stand for Christ's body and blood.

domus: A private, usually well-to-do townhouse.

"do ut des": "I, the mortal, give to you, the god, so that you may give back to me"; the term for the traditional contract between the gods and humans.

equestrians (or *equites*, or knights): A well-to-do class of Romans whose members earned their money through business and trade.

familia: Household; the family.

freedmen: Former slaves.

insulae **(singular is *insula*)**: An apartment block in a Roman city.

literate: Able to read and write.

materfamilias: The lady of a Roman household, usually the paterfamilias's wife.

pantheon: A group of gods worshiped by a people.

paterfamilias: The male head of a Roman household.

patronage: The social system in which one person, the client, did favors for a wealthier and more powerful person, the patron, in exchange for financial and legal protection.

persecute: To harass, injure, or otherwise oppress a person or a group, usually for reasons of race, nationality, religion, or sexual orientation.

sestertius **(plural** *sestertii* **or sesterces)**: A silver or bronze coin originally equal to 2.5 asses and later 4, and also .25 of a denarius.

specus: The water channel of a Roman aqueduct.

tolerant: Open to and accepting of other people's beliefs and customs.

vernae: Slaves who were born and grew up in the home.

villa: A large, usually comfortable country house.

For More Information

Books

Lionel Casson, *Daily Life in Ancient Rome*. New York: American Heritage, 1975. A well-written presentation of how the Romans lived, including their homes, streets, entertainment, foods, theaters, religion, slaves, marriage customs, and more.

Phil R. Cox and Annabel Spenceley, *Who Were the Romans?* Boston: EDC, 1994. An impressive, well-illustrated introduction to the Romans, presented in a question-and-answer format.

Anthony Marks and Graham Tingay, *The Romans.* London: Usborne, 1990. An excellent summary of the main aspects of Roman history, life, and arts, supported by hundreds of beautiful and accurate drawings reconstructing Roman times. Aimed at basic readers but highly recommended for anyone interested in Roman civilization.

Don Nardo, *Life of a Roman Slave*. San Diego: Lucent Books, 1998. A detailed and comprehensive, though easy-to-read, study of the institution of Roman slavery.
——— *Roman Mythology*: San Diego: KidHaven, 2002. Tells the major Roman myths in a format suitable for young readers.

Websites

Clients and Patrons, Discovery Channel
(http://myron.sjsu.edu/romeweb/SOCIAL/art2.htm).
An excellent overview of the Roman institution of patronage.

Roman Dress, Illustrated History of the Roman Empire
(www.roman-empire.net/society/soc-dress.htm).
A very informative site about everyday Roman clothing, supplemented by photos and drawings.

The Roman House, Illustrated History of the Roman Empire
(www.roman-empire.net/society/soc-house.html).
This site provides a ground plan of a typical Roman townhouse and gives detailed descriptions of each room.

Women in Roman Society, Discovery Channel
(http://myron.sjsu.edu/romeweb/LADYCONT/LADYCONT.htm).
Provides a long list of links, each leading to a biography of a noted Roman woman.

Index

Altars, 17, 27–28
Animals, 27–28
Aqueducts, 21, 22, 33–36, 37
Armies, 5
Atrium, 19
Auctoritas, 10
Augustus, 5, 9

Christianity, 28, 30–31
Cicero, 11, 17
City homes, 19–22
Civil rights, 6, 12
Class, social, 9–15
Clients, 14–15, 19
Country homes, 17–19

Domus, 19

Emperor, 6, 11, 31
Equestrians, 11
Estates, 10, 18

Family, 17, 22–23
Farms, 10, 17, 18
Festivals, 23, 26, 29
Freedmen, 12, 14
Freemen, 12

Gods, 7, 25–31
Government, 5
Greece, 26

Heritage, 17
Holidays, 23
Horace, 22
Houses, 17–23

Insulae, 21

Jesus of Nazareth, 30–31
Jobs, 11, 12, 14, 22–23
Judaism, 31
Juvenal, 15, 28

Kings, 5
Knights, 11

Language, 10
Latin, 10
Lower classes, 11, 12, 14, 15

Materfamilias, 22

Pantheon, 25–26
Paterfamilias, 22
Patricians, 10, 11, 12
Patronage system, 14–15
Pliny the Younger, 18–19, 20
Prayer, 27, 28

Religion, 7, 25–31
Republic, 5
Rituals, 27–28, 30
Roads, 36, 38–39
Roman Empire, 5–6, 9

Sacrifice, 27–28
Saturnalia, 23
Senate, 5, 11
Slaves, 12, 14, 17, 23, 35, 36
Social status, 9–15
Societies, 5–7
Spirits, 17, 25

Status, social, 9–15
Sunday, 28, 30

Temples, 26, 28, 29
Townhouse, 19

Upper classes, 10–11

Villas, 18, 20

Water, 21–22, 34–36
Wealth, 10, 14
Women, 6–7, 22–23
Worship, 27–28

Picture Credits

cover © The Art Archive/Musée du Louvre Paris/Dagli Orti; pages 4, 8, 26, 29, 34, 39 © Corel Corporation; pages 6, 12, 24 © Scala/Art Resource, NY; page 7 © Complete Encyclopedia of Illustration; pages 10, 11, 15, 23, 31 © North Wind Picture Archives; pages 13, 27 © Mary Evans Picture Library; pages 14, 36, 37 © Erich Lessing/Art Resource, NY; page 16 © Réunion des Musés Nationaux/Art Resources, NY; page 18 © Gilles Mermet/Art Resources, NY; page 19 © The Art Archive/Bibliothèque des Arts Décoratifs Paris/Dagli Orti; page 21 © The Art Archive/Museo della Civita romana rome/Dagli Orti; page 22 © Alinari/Art Resource, NY; page 30 © Joseph Paris Collection; page 32 © Mimmo Jodice/CORBIS; page 35 © Vanni Archive/CORBIS;

About the Author

Historian Don Nardo has published many volumes about ancient Roman history and culture, including *The Roman Empire*, *A Travel Guide to Ancient Rome*, and *Life of a Roman Gladiator*. He lives in Massachusetts with his wife, Christine.

1 - 11/06
10 - 3/16